Bible Reading Journal:
Rest and Be Refreshed

"Your Word is a lamp to my feet.
And a light to my path."
Psalm 119:105

This Journal Belongs to:

_____

"Again, the kingdom of heaven is like a merchant seeking fine pearls, and upon finding one pearl of great value, he went and sold all that he had and bought it."

Matthew 13:45-46

Copyright © 2019 Adriana Morales-Spokane
All rights reserved.

ISBN: 9781794685420

Scripture quotations taken from the **New American Standard Bible** © (NASB), Copyright © 1960, 1962, 1963, 1968, 1971, 1972, 1973, 1975, 1977, 1995 by The Lockman Foundation. Used by permission.
www.Lockman.org

DEDICATION

Abba Father,

You are a lighthouse in the midst of my distress. Your loving presence settles the rhythms of the open sea. Your promise is a fresh sea breeze to my soul. Your Word is an anchor to both mind and heart. Your Holy Spirit teaches me 'how to' navigate the journey. Your Wisdom helps me adjust the sails along the way.

Let us scuba dive and explore the treasures of the seas. The beauty of vivid coral reefs is awe-inspiring. You are the captain of all life adventures; I will never be lost again! You are a warm-hearted Father whose love never changes or ends.

You hear every beat of my heart!

Open your arms 'wide-open' and hold me close to your heart. Don't ever let me go. Thank you, Jesus, for being the sunrise of my troubled days. No troubles, disasters or tragedies in life will separate me from your bountiful love.

"nor height, nor depth, nor any other created thing, will be able to separate us from the love of God, which is in Christ Jesus our Lord."
Romans 8:39

Your forever travel companion, in Jesus' name,

I boldly praise. Amen

Love,

Your Beloved Child.

Welcome!

This Bible journal is a companion for your Bible Readings.

It will help you reflect and pray over selected Scriptures whether you are sitting at a kitchen table, taking a lunch break, waiting in line to pick-up your child from school or drinking a cup of coffee at a local cafe. This journal will provide you with ample journaling space to record your personal reflections when you read Bible passages for forty days.

You will find brief, written prompts that will guide you thru spiritual disciplines: Obedience, Forgiveness, Thanksgiving, and Prayer. This portable journal is perfect for anyone who tends to be busy throughout the day or travels often.

Adriana appreciates the journaling process. She renews her mind with His Word, strengthens her heart with His promises and refreshes her soul with His unfailing love and faithfulness.

Are you ready to establish these disciplines in your life? If so, your life will be transformed over the course of time. May the Holy Spirit be your best Counselor. I pray you rest in Jesus Christ and be refreshed in the next forty days.

Standing on Firm Grounds Today!

"Therefore, everyone who hears these words of Mine and acts on them, may be compared to a wise man who built his house on the rock. And the rain fell, and the floods came, and the winds blew and slammed against that house; and yet it did not fall, for it had been founded on the rock. Everyone who hears these words of Mine and does not act on them, will be like a foolish man who built his house on the sand. The rain fell, and the floods came, and the winds blew and slammed against that house; and it fell-and great was its fall." Matthew 7:24-27

Several years ago, I was standing on sinking ground with my Faith walk. Church attendance was 'hit or miss', bible reading was inconsistent, and prayerful life was non-existent. I was distant from the Lord. I was consumed by 'cultural busyness' and distracted by a fast-paced lifestyle. No margin for rest, adequate self-care or time for His Word.

Yes! You heard me right. I was standing on shaky territory.

I was a reckless woman who did not read or act on His Word. I was vulnerable and helpless. "Enemies of the heart" took root in my soul from paralyzing fear, doubt, hatred, unforgiveness, isolation to bitterness. I was resting at the bottom of the pit, 'darkness of depression', in the midst of loss and separation, and overwhelming life circumstances. I was grief-stricken with dad's sudden death, overwhelmed by a regional leadership platform and troubled by mom's relocation back to South America.

My world had drastically turned upside down in less than three months.

But God ...

He has never left me nor forsaken me.

When the Holy Spirit convicted me of His faithfulness, I immediately turned back to His Word one day at a time. Re-building an intimate relationship with the Lord was a gradual process yet it was worth the time and commitment.

Spiritual disciplines; repentance, forgiveness, thanksgiving, and prayer transformed my life one day at a time.

He is my Refuge, Comforter and the Best Counselor. He is my Rock today. The more I read and apply His Word to my everyday life, the closer I am to the Lord. His faithfulness, favor, and grace are evident, and His mercies never run out.

I am standing on a firm foundation today.

"You shall walk in all the way which the LORD your God has commanded you, that you may live and that it may be well with you, and that you may prolong your days in the land which you will possess." Deuteronomy 5:33

"by loving the LORD your God, by obeying His voice, and by holding fast to Him; for this is your life and the length of your days, that you may live in the land which the LORD swore to your fathers, to Abraham, Isaac, and Jacob, to give them.'" Deuteronomy 30:20

"The LORD is my rock and my fortress and my deliverer, My God, my rock, in whom I take refuge; My shield and the horn of my salvation, my stronghold."
Psalms 18:2

How to use this Journal?

This journal will assist you in recording your thoughts, reflections, and observations when reading your Bible passages. You may either be taking notes at Bible Study class, listening to a sermon in Church, at a conference, or even reading your Bible quietly in your home.

This journal will keep a record of 'how' the Lord speaks to you when actively engaged in His Word. It offers you forty Bible passages to encourage you to rest in Him and be refreshed with His promises. The additional journaling pages will invite you to an open forum so you may select Bible verses you would like to meditate on or even the ones you want to memorize over the course of the next forty days.

This journal gives you an opportunity to inscribe or write the Scripture(s). When writing verses, you will engage another one of your senses, touch. Research has proven that if you use more than one of your senses in any given activity, the impact will be greater and you will be able to remember the information for longer periods of time. I don't know about you my friend, but I experience great difficulties in memorizing His Word. Repetition has helped me over the years to hide His Truth in my heart (Proverbs 3:3).

Practical application of His Word is critical in our daily walk with Jesus Christ. As a matter of fact, His Truth reminds us of the following, "For if anyone is a hearer of the word and not a doer, he is like a man who looks at his natural face in a mirror; for once he has looked at himself and gone away, he has immediately forgotten what kind of person he was. But one who looks intently at the perfect laws, the law of liberty, and abides by it, not having become a forgetful hearer but an effectual doer, this man will be blessed in what he does." (James 1: 23-25)

God Bless your journaling experience in the next forty days and always your sister in Christ, Adriana.

Testimonies

"I am so encouraged when I pray for wisdom, strength and courage! I feel so much closer to God when I pray." ~ *Rob S.*

"My relationship with God is a growing priority in my life. I cannot walk, know, and experience his glorious presence, transforming power, unending love, and awesome grace without reading the Bible daily, praying at all times, confessing my sins and faults and giving thanks for everything. Building these disciplines helps me to focus on Jesus and his kingdom, to grow in my Christian faith, to become more mature, and to be more like Jesus." ~ *Angelica L.*

"Investing your time in God's Word and seeking His Will by prayer will reveal His Glorious Promises and Faithfulness."
~ *Charissa C.*

"Journaling has not only been therapeutic over the years but it has made a difference in my walk with Jesus.
Thanksgiving has renewed my mind, Prayer has strengthened my heart and soul, and Obedience has transformed my life! There is power in the Cross." ~ *Adriana M.*

Your Greatness is a Song of Hope

Heavenly Father,

You are our Lord and Savior. You died at the Cross, forgave those who sinned against you, and resurrected on the third day to offer us eternal life,

You are a Light to those who are blind-folded by temptations and a compass to those who are sleepless in the wilderness. You march closely with the broken-hearted, heal the wounds from past misfortunes, and revive our souls from shattered dreams,

You relentlessly maneuver the heights of steep mountains and execute magnificent, prized miracles in our ordinary lives!

You are a beacon in the midst of chaos and the matchless hope for today's helpless world,

You are worthy of praise, Abba Father (Psalm 145:3). Your generous hand is filled with promises and your heart sings distinct melodies of joy and hope, I'm telling the world about all the phenomenal acts you do every day. You are an amazing God!

Your never-ending grace, unfailing love, and unmerited favor to all generations are the manifestation of your deep love for us.

I want to witness your immeasurable greatness, power and strength in my life today and always. Since your 'heart tunes' are my song of joy and hope (Psalms 59:16), I'm asking for you to always be my refuge and fortress until my last breath on earth!

In Jesus' name, I boldly pray.

Amen

ACKNOWLEDGMENTS

To my beloved Jesus, thank you for being graceful, faithful and forgiving all of these years particularly when I was rebellious, lost, distant and at "the end of my rope."

To my beloved folks, thank you both for being loving, tolerant, accepting and unconditional.

To my beloved husband, thank you for being supportive, understanding and willing to embrace a journey in Christ for years to come.

To my friends, thank you for giving me an opportunity to share life with you one moment at a time, and for teaching me valuable lessons in 'how to' connect with today's world.

To my nieces, nephews, great-nieces, great-nephews and those to come, thank you for being family, and my prayer is for our hearts to connect intimately in the future regardless of geographical barriers.

**"Open my eyes, that I may behold
Wonderful things from Your law."**
Psalm 119:18

Date: _____

Selected Bible Passage: "Thus the heavens and the earth were completed, and all their hosts. By the seventh day God completed His work which He had done, and He rested on the seventh day from all His work which He had done. Then God blessed the seventh day and sanctified it, because in it He rested from all His work which God had created made." Genesis 2: 1-3

Reflections or Observations:

_____
_____
_____
_____
_____

Inscribe the Selected Verse(s):

_____
_____
_____
_____
_____
_____
_____
_____
_____
_____
_____
_____
_____
_____
_____

But He said, "On the contrary, blessed are those who hear the word of God and observe it." Luke 11:28

Lord, help me step out in obedience today…

_____
_____
_____

"But a man must examine himself, and in so doing he is to eat of the bread and drink of the cup." 1 Corinthians 11:28

Lord, I would like to share and repent…

_____
_____
_____

"For if you forgive others for their transgressions, your heavenly Father will also forgive you." Matthew 6:14

Lord, I need to forgive…

_____
_____
_____

"O taste and see that the LORD is good; How blessed is the man who takes refuge in Him!" Psalm 34:8

Lord, I praise You for today's blessings...

_____
_____
_____

"Ask, and it will be given to you; seek, and you will find; knock, and it will be opened to you." Matthew 7:7

Lord, hear my prayers …

_____
_____
_____
_____
_____
_____
_____

"Open my eyes, that I may behold Wonderful things from Your law."
Psalm 119:18

Date: _____

Selected Bible Passage:
"Therefore, let us draw near with confidence to the throne of grace, so that we may receive mercy and find grace to help in time of need." Hebrews 4:16

Reflections or Observations:
_____
_____
_____
_____
_____

Inscribe the Selected Verse(s):
_____
_____
_____
_____
_____
_____
_____
_____
_____
_____
_____
_____

But He said, "On the contrary, blessed are those who hear the word of God and observe it." Luke 11:28

Lord, help me step out in obedience today…

_____
_____
_____

"But a man must examine himself, and in so doing he is to eat of the bread and drink of the cup." 1 Corinthians 11:28

Lord, I would like to share and repent…

_____
_____
_____

"For if you forgive others for their transgressions, your heavenly Father will also forgive you." Matthew 6:14

Lord, I need to forgive…

_____
_____
_____

"O taste and see that the LORD is good; How blessed is the man who takes refuge in Him!" Psalm 34:8

Lord, I praise You for today's blessings...

_____
_____
_____

"Ask, and it will be given to you; seek, and you will find; knock, and it will be opened to you." Matthew 7:7

Lord, hear my prayers …

_____
_____
_____
_____
_____
_____

"Open my eyes, that I may behold Wonderful things from Your law."
Psalm 119:18

Date: _____

Selected Bible Passage: "But You, O LORD, are a shield about me, my glory, and the One who lifts my head. I was crying to the LORD with my voice, and He answered me from His holy mountain. Selah. I lay down and slept; I awoke, for the Lord sustains me." Psalm 3:3-5

Reflections or Observations:

_____

_____

_____

Inscribe the Selected Verse(s):

_____

_____

_____

_____

_____

_____

But He said, "On the contrary, blessed are those who hear the word of God and observe it." Luke 11:28

Lord, help me step out in obedience today…

_____
_____
_____

"But a man must examine himself, and in so doing he is to eat of the bread and drink of the cup." 1 Corinthians 11:28

Lord, I would like to share and repent…

_____
_____
_____

"For if you forgive others for their transgressions, your heavenly Father will also forgive you." Matthew 6:14

Lord, I need to forgive…

_____
_____
_____

"O taste and see that the LORD is good; How blessed is the man who takes refuge in Him!" Psalm 34:8

Lord, I praise You for today's blessings...

_____
_____
_____

"Ask, and it will be given to you; seek, and you will find; knock, and it will be opened to you." Matthew 7:7

Lord, hear my prayers …

_____
_____
_____
_____
_____
_____
_____

**"Open my eyes, that I may behold
Wonderful things from Your law."**
Psalm 119:18

Date: _____

Selected Bible Passage: "Finally, be strong in the Lord and in the strength of His might." Ephesians 6:10

Reflections or Observations:
_____
_____
_____
_____
_____

Inscribe the Selected Verse(s):
_____
_____
_____
_____
_____
_____
_____
_____
_____
_____
_____
_____
_____

But He said, "On the contrary, blessed are those who hear the word of God and observe it." Luke 11:28

Lord, help me step out in obedience today…

_____
_____
_____

"But a man must examine himself, and in so doing he is to eat of the bread and drink of the cup." 1 Corinthians 11:28

Lord, I would like to share and repent…

_____
_____
_____

"For if you forgive others for their transgressions, your heavenly Father will also forgive you." Matthew 6:14

Lord, I need to forgive…

_____
_____
_____

"O taste and see that the LORD is good; How blessed is the man who takes refuge in Him!" Psalm 34:8

Lord, I praise You for today's blessings...

_____
_____
_____

"Ask, and it will be given to you; seek, and you will find; knock, and it will be opened to you." Matthew 7:7

Lord, hear my prayers …

_____
_____
_____
_____
_____
_____

**"Open my eyes, that I may behold
Wonderful things from Your law."**
Psalm 119:18

Date: _____

Selected Bible Passage: "The steadfast of mind You will keep in perfect peace, because he trusts in You. Trust in the Lord forever, For in GOD the LORD, *we have* an everlasting Rock." Isaiah 26:3-4

Reflections or Observations:

_____
_____
_____
_____

Inscribe the Selected Verse(s):

_____
_____
_____
_____
_____
_____
_____
_____
_____
_____
_____
_____

But He said, "On the contrary, blessed are those who hear the word of God and observe it." Luke 11:28

Lord, help me step out in obedience today…

_____
_____
_____

"But a man must examine himself, and in so doing he is to eat of the bread and drink of the cup." 1 Corinthians 11:28

Lord, I would like to share and repent…

_____
_____
_____

"For if you forgive others for their transgressions, your heavenly Father will also forgive you." Matthew 6:14

Lord, I need to forgive…

_____
_____
_____

"O taste and see that the LORD is good; How blessed is the man who takes refuge in Him!" Psalm 34:8

Lord, I praise You for today's blessings...

_____
_____
_____

"Ask, and it will be given to you; seek, and you will find; knock, and it will be opened to you." Matthew 7:7

Lord, hear my prayers …

_____
_____
_____
_____
_____
_____
_____

"Open my eyes, that I may behold Wonderful things from Your law."
Psalm 119:18

Date: _____

Selected Bible Passage: "Now on the last day, the great *day* of the feast, Jesus stood and cried out, saying, "If anyone is thirsty, let him come to Me and drink. He who believes in Me, as the Scripture said, 'From his innermost being will flow rivers of living water." John 7: 37-38

Reflections or Observations:
_____
_____
_____
_____
_____

Inscribe the Selected Verse(s):
_____
_____
_____
_____
_____
_____
_____
_____
_____
_____
_____
_____

But He said, "On the contrary, blessed are those who hear the word of God and observe it." Luke 11:28

Lord, help me step out in obedience today…

_____
_____
_____

"But a man must examine himself, and in so doing he is to eat of the bread and drink of the cup." 1 Corinthians 11:28

Lord, I would like to share and repent…

_____
_____
_____

"For if you forgive others for their transgressions, your heavenly Father will also forgive you." Matthew 6:14

Lord, I need to forgive…

_____
_____
_____

"O taste and see that the LORD is good; How blessed is the man who takes refuge in Him!" Psalm 34:8

Lord, I praise You for today's blessings...

_____
_____
_____

"Ask, and it will be given to you; seek, and you will find; knock, and it will be opened to you." Matthew 7:7

Lord, hear my prayers …

_____
_____
_____
_____
_____
_____

"Open my eyes, that I may behold Wonderful things from Your law."
Psalm 119:18

Date: _____

Selected Bible Passage: "Because of the devastation of the afflicted, because of the groaning of the needy. Now I will arise," says the LORD; "I will set him in the safety for which he longs. "The words of the LORD are pure words. As silver tried in a furnace on the earth, refined seven times. You, O LORD, will keep them; You will preserve him from this generation forever." Psalm 12:5-7

Reflections or Observations:

_____
_____
_____

Inscribe the Selected Verse(s):

_____
_____
_____
_____
_____
_____

But He said, "On the contrary, blessed are those who hear the word of God and observe it." Luke 11:28

Lord, help me step out in obedience today…

_____
_____
_____

"But a man must examine himself, and in so doing he is to eat of the bread and drink of the cup." 1 Corinthians 11:28

Lord, I would like to share and repent…

_____
_____
_____

"For if you forgive others for their transgressions, your heavenly Father will also forgive you." Matthew 6:14

Lord, I need to forgive…

_____
_____
_____

"O taste and see that the LORD is good; How blessed is the man who takes refuge in Him!" Psalm 34:8

Lord, I praise You for today's blessings...

_____
_____
_____

"Ask, and it will be given to you; seek, and you will find; knock, and it will be opened to you." Matthew 7:7

Lord, hear my prayers …

_____
_____
_____
_____
_____
_____

> **"Open my eyes, that I may behold**
> **Wonderful things from Your law."**
> Psalm 119:18

Date: _____

Selected Bible Passage: "The LORD is my shepherd, I shall not want. He makes me lie down in green pastures; He leads me beside quiet waters. He restores my soul; He guides me in the paths of righteousness for His name's sake." Psalm 23:1-3

Reflections or Observations:
_____
_____
_____
_____
_____

Inscribe the Selected Verse(s):
_____
_____
_____
_____
_____
_____
_____
_____
_____
_____
_____
_____

But He said, "On the contrary, blessed are those who hear the word of God and observe it." Luke 11:28

Lord, help me step out in obedience today…

_____
_____
_____

"But a man must examine himself, and in so doing he is to eat of the bread and drink of the cup." 1 Corinthians 11:28

Lord, I would like to share and repent…

_____
_____
_____

"For if you forgive others for their transgressions, your heavenly Father will also forgive you." Matthew 6:14

Lord, I need to forgive…

_____
_____
_____

"O taste and see that the LORD is good; How blessed is the man who takes refuge in Him!" Psalm 34:8

Lord, I praise You for today's blessings…

_____
_____
_____

"Ask, and it will be given to you; seek, and you will find; knock, and it will be opened to you." Matthew 7:7

Lord, hear my prayers …

_____
_____
_____
_____
_____
_____
_____

> **"Open my eyes, that I may behold Wonderful things from Your law."**
> Psalm 119:18

Date: _____

Selected Bible Passage: "Come to Me, all who are weary and heavy-laden, and I will give you rest. Take My yoke upon you and learn from Me, for I am gentle and humble in heart, and YOU WILL FIND REST FOR YOUR SOULS. For My yoke is easy and My burden is light." Matthew 11:28-30

Reflections or Observations:
_____
_____
_____
_____
_____

Inscribe the Selected Verse(s):
_____
_____
_____
_____
_____
_____
_____
_____
_____
_____
_____
_____

But He said, "On the contrary, blessed are those who hear the word of God and observe it." Luke 11:28

Lord, help me step out in obedience today…

_____
_____
_____

"But a man must examine himself, and in so doing he is to eat of the bread and drink of the cup." 1 Corinthians 11:28

Lord, I would like to share and repent…

_____
_____
_____

"For if you forgive others for their transgressions, your heavenly Father will also forgive you." Matthew 6:14

Lord, I need to forgive…

_____
_____
_____

"O taste and see that the LORD is good; How blessed is the man who takes refuge in Him!" Psalm 34:8

Lord, I praise You for today's blessings...

_____
_____
_____

"Ask, and it will be given to you; seek, and you will find; knock, and it will be opened to you." Matthew 7:7

Lord, hear my prayers …

_____
_____
_____
_____
_____
_____
_____

"Open my eyes, that I may behold Wonderful things from Your law."
Psalm 119:18

D Date: _____

S Selected Bible Passage: "My soul *waits* in silence for God only; From Him is my salvation. He only is my rock and my salvation, my stronghold; I shall not be greatly shaken" Psalm 62:1-2

R Reflections or Observations:
_____
_____
_____
_____
_____

I Inscribe the Selected Verse(s):
_____
_____
_____
_____
_____
_____
_____
_____
_____
_____
_____
_____

But He said, "On the contrary, blessed are those who hear the word of God and observe it." Luke 11:28

Lord, help me step out in obedience today…

_____
_____
_____

"But a man must examine himself, and in so doing he is to eat of the bread and drink of the cup." 1 Corinthians 11:28

Lord, I would like to share and repent…

_____
_____
_____

"For if you forgive others for their transgressions, your heavenly Father will also forgive you." Matthew 6:14

Lord, I need to forgive…

_____
_____
_____

**"O taste and see that the LORD is good;
How blessed is the man who takes refuge in Him!"** Psalm 34:8

Lord, I praise You for today's blessings...

_____
_____
_____

"Ask, and it will be given to you; seek, and you will find; knock, and it will be opened to you." Matthew 7:7

Lord, hear my prayers …

_____
_____
_____
_____
_____
_____
_____

**"Open my eyes, that I may behold
Wonderful things from Your law."**
Psalm 119:18

Date: _____

Selected Bible Passage: "One hand full of rest is better than two fists full of labor and striving after wind." Ecclesiastes 4:6

Reflections or Observations:
_____
_____
_____
_____
_____

Inscribe the Selected Verse(s):
_____
_____
_____
_____
_____
_____
_____
_____
_____
_____
_____
_____
_____

But He said, "On the contrary, blessed are those who hear the word of God and observe it." Luke 11:28

Lord, help me step out in obedience today…

_____
_____
_____

"But a man must examine himself, and in so doing he is to eat of the bread and drink of the cup." 1 Corinthians 11:28

Lord, I would like to share and repent…

_____
_____
_____

"For if you forgive others for their transgressions, your heavenly Father will also forgive you." Matthew 6:14

Lord, I need to forgive…

_____
_____
_____

**"O taste and see that the LORD is good;
How blessed is the man who takes refuge in Him!"** Psalm 34:8

Lord, I praise You for today's blessings...

_____
_____
_____

"Ask, and it will be given to you; seek, and you will find; knock, and it will be opened to you." Matthew 7:7

Lord, hear my prayers …

_____
_____
_____
_____
_____
_____

**"Open my eyes, that I may behold
Wonderful things from Your law."**
Psalm 119:18

Date: _____

Selected Bible Passage: "Rest in the LORD and wait patiently for Him; Do not fret because of him who prospers in his way, Because of the man who carries out wicked schemes. Cease from anger and forsake wrath; Do not fret; *it leads* only to evildoing. For evildoers will be cut off, but those who wait for the LORD, they will inherit the land." Psalm 37:7-9

Reflections or Observations:

_____
_____
_____
_____

Inscribe the Selected Verse(s):

_____
_____
_____
_____
_____

But He said, "On the contrary, blessed are those who hear the word of God and observe it." Luke 11:28

Lord, help me step out in obedience today…

_____
_____
_____

"But a man must examine himself, and in so doing he is to eat of the bread and drink of the cup." 1 Corinthians 11:28

Lord, I would like to share and repent…

_____
_____
_____

"For if you forgive others for their transgressions, your heavenly Father will also forgive you." Matthew 6:14

Lord, I need to forgive…

_____
_____
_____

**"O taste and see that the LORD is good;
How blessed is the man who takes refuge in Him!"** Psalm 34:8

Lord, I praise You for today's blessings...

_____
_____
_____

"Ask, and it will be given to you; seek, and you will find; knock, and it will be opened to you." Matthew 7:7

Lord, hear my prayers …

_____
_____
_____
_____
_____
_____

> **"Open my eyes, that I may behold
> Wonderful things from Your law."**
> Psalm 119:18

Date: _____

Selected Bible Passage: "The Spirit of the LORD will rest on Him, the spirit of wisdom and understanding, the spirit of counsel and strength, the spirit of knowledge and the fear of the LORD." Isaiah 11:2

Reflections or Observations:

_____
_____
_____
_____

Inscribe the Selected Verse(s):

_____
_____
_____
_____
_____
_____
_____
_____
_____
_____
_____

But He said, "On the contrary, blessed are those who hear the word of God and observe it." Luke 11:28

Lord, help me step out in obedience today…

_____
_____
_____

"But a man must examine himself, and in so doing he is to eat of the bread and drink of the cup." 1 Corinthians 11:28

Lord, I would like to share and repent…

_____
_____
_____

"For if you forgive others for their transgressions, your heavenly Father will also forgive you." Matthew 6:14

Lord, I need to forgive…

_____
_____
_____

**"O taste and see that the L<small>ORD</small> is good;
How blessed is the man who takes refuge in Him!"** Psalm 34:8

Lord, I praise You for today's blessings…

_____
_____
_____

"Ask, and it will be given to you; seek, and you will find; knock, and it will be opened to you." Matthew 7:7

Lord, hear my prayers …

_____
_____
_____
_____
_____
_____
_____

> "Open my eyes, that I may behold
> Wonderful things from Your law."
> Psalm 119:18

Date: _____

Selected Bible Passage: "Do not worry then, saying, 'What will we eat?' or 'What will we drink?' or 'What will we wear for clothing?' For the Gentiles eagerly seek all these things; for your heavenly Father knows that you need all these things. But seek first His kingdom and His righteousness, and all these things will be added to you." Matthew 6:31-33

Reflections or Observations:

_____
_____
_____
_____

Inscribe the Selected Verse(s):

_____
_____
_____
_____
_____
_____
_____
_____
_____
_____
_____
_____

But He said, "On the contrary, blessed are those who hear the word of God and observe it." Luke 11:28

Lord, help me step out in obedience today…

_____
_____
_____

"But a man must examine himself, and in so doing he is to eat of the bread and drink of the cup." 1 Corinthians 11:28

Lord, I would like to share and repent…

_____
_____
_____

"For if you forgive others for their transgressions, your heavenly Father will also forgive you." Matthew 6:14

Lord, I need to forgive…

_____
_____
_____

**"O taste and see that the LORD is good;
How blessed is the man who takes refuge in Him!"** Psalm 34:8

Lord, I praise You for today's blessings...

_____
_____
_____

"Ask, and it will be given to you; seek, and you will find; knock, and it will be opened to you." Matthew 7:7

Lord, hear my prayers …

_____
_____
_____
_____
_____
_____
_____

**"Open my eyes, that I may behold
Wonderful things from Your law."**
Psalm 119:18

Date: _____

Selected Bible Passage:
"So, do not worry about tomorrow; for tomorrow will care for itself. Each day has enough trouble of its own." Matthew 6:34

Reflections or Observations:
_____
_____
_____
_____
_____

Inscribe the Selected Verse(s):
_____
_____
_____
_____
_____
_____
_____
_____
_____
_____
_____

But He said, "On the contrary, blessed are those who hear the word of God and observe it." Luke 11:28

Lord, help me step out in obedience today…

_____
_____
_____

"But a man must examine himself, and in so doing he is to eat of the bread and drink of the cup." 1 Corinthians 11:28

Lord, I would like to share and repent…

_____
_____
_____

"For if you forgive others for their transgressions, your heavenly Father will also forgive you." Matthew 6:14

Lord, I need to forgive…

_____
_____
_____

"O taste and see that the LORD is good; How blessed is the man who takes refuge in Him!" Psalm 34:8

Lord, I praise You for today's blessings...

_____
_____
_____

"Ask, and it will be given to you; seek, and you will find; knock, and it will be opened to you." Matthew 7:7

Lord, hear my prayers …

_____
_____
_____
_____
_____
_____

**"Open my eyes, that I may behold
Wonderful things from Your law."**
Psalm 119:18

Date: _____

Selected Bible Passage: "Grace to you and peace from God our Father and the Lord Jesus Christ, who gave Himself for our sins so that He might rescue us from this present evil age, according to the will of our God and Father, to whom *be* the glory forevermore. Amen." Galatians 1:3-5

Reflections or Observations:
_____
_____
_____
_____
_____

Inscribe the Selected Verse(s):
_____
_____
_____
_____
_____
_____
_____
_____
_____
_____
_____

But He said, "On the contrary, blessed are those who hear the word of God and observe it." Luke 11:28

Lord, help me step out in obedience today…

_____
_____
_____

"But a man must examine himself, and in so doing he is to eat of the bread and drink of the cup." 1 Corinthians 11:28

Lord, I would like to share and repent…

_____
_____
_____

"For if you forgive others for their transgressions, your heavenly Father will also forgive you." Matthew 6:14

Lord, I need to forgive…

_____
_____
_____

**"O taste and see that the LORD is good;
How blessed is the man who takes refuge in Him!"** Psalm 34:8

Lord, I praise You for today's blessings…

_____
_____
_____

"Ask, and it will be given to you; seek, and you will find; knock, and it will be opened to you." Matthew 7:7

Lord, hear my prayers …

_____
_____
_____
_____
_____
_____
_____

**"Open my eyes, that I may behold
Wonderful things from Your law."**
Psalm 119:18

Date: _____

Selected Bible Passage: "And which of you by worrying can add a *single* hour to his life's span? If then you cannot do even a very little thing, why do you worry about other matters? Consider the lilies, how they grow: they neither toil nor spin; but I tell you, not even Solomon in all his glory clothed himself like one of these. But if God so clothes the grass in the field, which is *alive* today and tomorrow is thrown into the furnace, how much more *will He clothe* you? You men of little faith!" Luke 12:25-28

Reflections or Observations:

_____
_____
_____
_____

Inscribe the Selected Verse(s):

_____
_____
_____
_____
_____
_____
_____
_____

But He said, "On the contrary, blessed are those who hear the word of God and observe it." Luke 11:28

Lord, help me step out in obedience today…

_____
_____
_____

"But a man must examine himself, and in so doing he is to eat of the bread and drink of the cup." 1 Corinthians 11:28

Lord, I would like to share and repent…

_____
_____
_____

"For if you forgive others for their transgressions, your heavenly Father will also forgive you." Matthew 6:14

Lord, I need to forgive…

_____
_____
_____

"O taste and see that the LORD is good;
How blessed is the man who takes refuge in Him!" Psalm 34:8

Lord, I praise You for today's blessings...

_____
_____
_____

"Ask, and it will be given to you; seek, and you will find; knock, and it will be opened to you." Matthew 7:7

Lord, hear my prayers …

_____
_____
_____
_____
_____
_____
_____

**"Open my eyes, that I may behold
Wonderful things from Your law."**
Psalm 119:18

Date: _____

Selected Bible Passage: "For if Joshua had given them rest, He would not have spoken of another day after that. So there remains a Sabbath rest for the people of God. 1For the one who has entered His rest has himself also rested from his works, as God did from His. Therefore, let us be diligent to enter that rest, so that no one will fall, through *following* the same example of disobedience." Hebrews 4:8-12

Reflections or Observations:
_____
_____
_____
_____
_____

Inscribe the Selected Verse(s):
_____
_____
_____
_____
_____
_____
_____
_____
_____

But He said, "On the contrary, blessed are those who hear the word of God and observe it." Luke 11:28

Lord, help me step out in obedience today…

_____
_____
_____

"But a man must examine himself, and in so doing he is to eat of the bread and drink of the cup." 1 Corinthians 11:28

Lord, I would like to share and repent…

_____
_____
_____

"For if you forgive others for their transgressions, your heavenly Father will also forgive you." Matthew 6:14

Lord, I need to forgive…

_____
_____
_____

**"O taste and see that the LORD is good;
How blessed is the man who takes refuge in Him!"** Psalm 34:8

Lord, I praise You for today's blessings...

_____
_____
_____

"Ask, and it will be given to you; seek, and you will find; knock, and it will be opened to you." Matthew 7:7

Lord, hear my prayers …

_____
_____
_____
_____
_____
_____

**"Open my eyes, that I may behold
Wonderful things from Your law."**
Psalm 119:18

Date: _____

Selected Bible Passage: "Now on the last day, the great day of the feast, Jesus stood and cried out, saying, "If anyone is thirsty, let him come to Me and drink. He who believes in Me, as the Scripture said, 'From his innermost being will flow rivers of living water." John 7:37-38

Reflections or Observations:

_____
_____
_____
_____
_____

Inscribe the Selected Verse(s):

_____
_____
_____
_____
_____
_____
_____
_____
_____
_____
_____
_____

But He said, "On the contrary, blessed are those who hear the word of God and observe it." Luke 11:28

Lord, help me step out in obedience today…

_____
_____
_____

"But a man must examine himself, and in so doing he is to eat of the bread and drink of the cup." 1 Corinthians 11:28

Lord, I would like to share and repent…

_____
_____
_____

"For if you forgive others for their transgressions, your heavenly Father will also forgive you." Matthew 6:14

Lord, I need to forgive…

_____
_____
_____

"O taste and see that the LORD is good; How blessed is the man who takes refuge in Him!" Psalm 34:8

Lord, I praise You for today's blessings...

_____
_____
_____

"Ask, and it will be given to you; seek, and you will find; knock, and it will be opened to you." Matthew 7:7

Lord, hear my prayers …

_____
_____
_____
_____
_____
_____
_____

**"Open my eyes, that I may behold
Wonderful things from Your law."**
Psalm 119:18

Date: _____

Selected Bible Passage: "Know therefore that the LORD your God, He is God, the faithful God, who keeps His covenant and His lovingkindness to a thousandth generation with those who love Him and keep His commandments." Deuteronomy 7:9

Reflections or Observations:

_____
_____
_____
_____
_____

Inscribe the Selected Verse(s):

_____
_____
_____
_____
_____
_____
_____
_____
_____
_____

But He said, "On the contrary, blessed are those who hear the word of God and observe it." Luke 11:28

Lord, help me step out in obedience today...

___
___
___

"But a man must examine himself, and in so doing he is to eat of the bread and drink of the cup." 1 Corinthians 11:28

Lord, I would like to share and repent...

___
___
___

"For if you forgive others for their transgressions, your heavenly Father will also forgive you." Matthew 6:14

Lord, I need to forgive...

___
___
___

"O taste and see that the LORD is good; How blessed is the man who takes refuge in Him!" Psalm 34:8

Lord, I praise You for today's blessings...

___
___
___

"Ask, and it will be given to you; seek, and you will find; knock, and it will be opened to you." Matthew 7:7

Lord, hear my prayers ...

___
___
___
___
___
___

> "Open my eyes, that I may behold
> Wonderful things from Your law."
> Psalm 119:18

Date: _____

Selected Bible Passage: "The Rock! His work is perfect, For all His ways are just; A God of faithfulness and without injustice, Righteous and upright is He." Deuteronomy 32:4

Reflections or Observations:
_____
_____
_____
_____
_____

Inscribe the Selected Verse(s):
_____
_____
_____
_____
_____
_____
_____
_____
_____
_____
_____
_____

But He said, "On the contrary, blessed are those who hear the word of God and observe it." Luke 11:28

Lord, help me step out in obedience today…

_____
_____
_____

"But a man must examine himself, and in so doing he is to eat of the bread and drink of the cup." 1 Corinthians 11:28

Lord, I would like to share and repent…

_____
_____
_____

"For if you forgive others for their transgressions, your heavenly Father will also forgive you." Matthew 6:14

Lord, I need to forgive…

_____
_____
_____

"O taste and see that the LORD is good; How blessed is the man who takes refuge in Him!" Psalm 34:8

Lord, I praise You for today's blessings…

_____
_____
_____

"Ask, and it will be given to you; seek, and you will find; knock, and it will be opened to you." Matthew 7:7

Lord, hear my prayers …

_____
_____
_____
_____
_____
_____

**"Open my eyes, that I may behold
Wonderful things from Your law."**
Psalm 119:18

Date: _____

Selected Bible Passage: "Then Jesus again spoke to them, saying, "I am the Light of the world; he who follows Me will not walk in the darkness, but will have the Light of life." John 8:12

Reflections or Observations:
_____
_____
_____
_____
_____

Inscribe the Selected Verse(s):
_____
_____
_____
_____
_____
_____
_____
_____
_____
_____

But He said, "On the contrary, blessed are those who hear the word of God and observe it." Luke 11:28

Lord, help me step out in obedience today…

_____
_____
_____

"But a man must examine himself, and in so doing he is to eat of the bread and drink of the cup." 1 Corinthians 11:28

Lord, I would like to share and repent…

_____
_____
_____

"For if you forgive others for their transgressions, your heavenly Father will also forgive you." Matthew 6:14

Lord, I need to forgive…

_____
_____
_____

"O taste and see that the LORD is good; How blessed is the man who takes refuge in Him!" Psalm 34:8

Lord, I praise You for today's blessings...

_____
_____
_____

"Ask, and it will be given to you; seek, and you will find; knock, and it will be opened to you." Matthew 7:7

Lord, hear my prayers …

_____
_____
_____
_____
_____
_____

**"Open my eyes, that I may behold
Wonderful things from Your law."**
Psalm 119:18

D Date: _____

S Selected Bible Passage: "So, Jesus was saying to those Jews who had believed Him, "If you continue in My word, *then* you are truly disciples of Mine; and you will know the truth, and the truth will make you free." John 8: 31-32

R Reflections or Observations:
_____
_____
_____
_____
_____

I Inscribe the Selected Verse(s):
_____
_____
_____
_____
_____
_____
_____
_____
_____
_____
_____

But He said, "On the contrary, blessed are those who hear the word of God and observe it." Luke 11:28

Lord, help me step out in obedience today…

_____
_____
_____

"But a man must examine himself, and in so doing he is to eat of the bread and drink of the cup." 1 Corinthians 11:28

Lord, I would like to share and repent…

_____
_____
_____

"For if you forgive others for their transgressions, your heavenly Father will also forgive you." Matthew 6:14

Lord, I need to forgive…

_____
_____
_____

"O taste and see that the LORD is good; How blessed is the man who takes refuge in Him!" Psalm 34:8

Lord, I praise You for today's blessings...

_____
_____
_____

"Ask, and it will be given to you; seek, and you will find; knock, and it will be opened to you." Matthew 7:7

Lord, hear my prayers …

_____
_____
_____
_____
_____
_____
_____

**"Open my eyes, that I may behold
Wonderful things from Your law."**
Psalm 119:18

Date: _____

Selected Bible Passage: "Therefore there is now no condemnation for those who are in Christ Jesus. For the law of the Spirit of life in Christ Jesus has set you free from the law of sin and of death." Romans 8: 1-2

Reflections or Observations:
_____
_____
_____
_____
_____

Inscribe the Selected Verse(s):
_____
_____
_____
_____
_____
_____
_____
_____
_____
_____
_____

But He said, "On the contrary, blessed are those who hear the word of God and observe it." Luke 11:28

Lord, help me step out in obedience today…

_____
_____
_____

"But a man must examine himself, and in so doing he is to eat of the bread and drink of the cup." 1 Corinthians 11:28

Lord, I would like to share and repent…

_____
_____
_____

"For if you forgive others for their transgressions, your heavenly Father will also forgive you." Matthew 6:14

Lord, I need to forgive…

_____
_____
_____

"O taste and see that the LORD** is good; How blessed is the man who takes refuge in Him!"** Psalm 34:8

Lord, I praise You for today's blessings…

_____
_____
_____

"Ask, and it will be given to you; seek, and you will find; knock, and it will be opened to you." Matthew 7:7

Lord, hear my prayers …

_____
_____
_____
_____
_____
_____
_____

"Open my eyes, that I may behold Wonderful things from Your law."
Psalm 119:18

Date: _____

Selected Bible Passage: "But I have trusted in Your lovingkindness; My heart shall rejoice in Your salvation. I will sing to the LORD, Because He has dealt bountifully with me." Psalm 13:5-6

Reflections or Observations:
_____
_____
_____
_____
_____

Inscribe the Selected Verse(s):
_____
_____
_____
_____
_____
_____
_____
_____
_____
_____
_____
_____

But He said, "On the contrary, blessed are those who hear the word of God and observe it." Luke 11:28

Lord, help me step out in obedience today…
_____
_____
_____

"But a man must examine himself, and in so doing he is to eat of the bread and drink of the cup." 1 Corinthians 11:28

Lord, I would like to share and repent…
_____
_____
_____

"For if you forgive others for their transgressions, your heavenly Father will also forgive you." Matthew 6:14

Lord, I need to forgive…
_____
_____
_____

"O taste and see that the LORD is good; How blessed is the man who takes refuge in Him!" Psalm 34:8

Lord, I praise You for today's blessings...
_____
_____
_____

"Ask, and it will be given to you; seek, and you will find; knock, and it will be opened to you." Matthew 7:7

Lord, hear my prayers …
_____
_____
_____
_____
_____
_____

**"Open my eyes, that I may behold
Wonderful things from Your law."**
Psalm 119:18

Date: _____

Selected Bible Passage: "And God is able to make all grace abound to you, so that always having all sufficiency in everything, you may have an abundance for every good deed." 2 Corinthians 9:8

Reflections or Observations:
_____
_____
_____
_____
_____

Inscribe the Selected Verse(s):
_____
_____
_____
_____
_____
_____
_____
_____
_____
_____
_____
_____

> But He said, "On the contrary, blessed are those who hear the word of God and observe it." Luke 11:28

Lord, help me step out in obedience today…

_____
_____
_____

> "But a man must examine himself, and in so doing he is to eat of the bread and drink of the cup." 1 Corinthians 11:28

Lord, I would like to share and repent…

_____
_____
_____

> "For if you forgive others for their transgressions, your heavenly Father will also forgive you." Matthew 6:14

Lord, I need to forgive…

_____
_____
_____

> "O taste and see that the LORD is good; How blessed is the man who takes refuge in Him!" Psalm 34:8

Lord, I praise You for today's blessings...

_____
_____
_____

> "Ask, and it will be given to you; seek, and you will find; knock, and it will be opened to you." Matthew 7:7

Lord, hear my prayers …

_____
_____
_____
_____
_____
_____
_____

"Open my eyes, that I may behold Wonderful things from Your law."
Psalm 119:18

Date: _____

Selected Bible Passage:
"O taste and see that the LORD is good; How blessed is the man who takes refuge in Him!" Psalm 34:8

Reflections or Observations:
_____
_____
_____
_____
_____

Inscribe the Selected Verse(s):
_____
_____
_____
_____
_____
_____
_____
_____
_____
_____
_____
_____

But He said, "On the contrary, blessed are those who hear the word of God and observe it." Luke 11:28

Lord, help me step out in obedience today…

_____
_____
_____

"But a man must examine himself, and in so doing he is to eat of the bread and drink of the cup." 1 Corinthians 11:28

Lord, I would like to share and repent…

_____
_____
_____

"For if you forgive others for their transgressions, your heavenly Father will also forgive you." Matthew 6:14

Lord, I need to forgive…

_____
_____
_____

"O taste and see that the LORD is good; How blessed is the man who takes refuge in Him!" Psalm 34:8

Lord, I praise You for today's blessings...

_____
_____
_____

"Ask, and it will be given to you; seek, and you will find; knock, and it will be opened to you." Matthew 7:7

Lord, hear my prayers …

_____
_____
_____
_____
_____
_____
_____

**"Open my eyes, that I may behold
Wonderful things from Your law."**
Psalm 119:18

Date: _____

Selected Bible Passage:
"Whom have I in heaven *but You?* And besides You, I desire nothing on earth. My flesh and my heart may fail, But God is the strength of my heart and my portion forever." Psalm 73:25-26

Reflections or Observations:
_____
_____
_____
_____

Inscribe the Selected Verse(s):
_____
_____
_____
_____
_____
_____
_____
_____
_____
_____
_____
_____

But He said, "On the contrary, blessed are those who hear the word of God and observe it." Luke 11:28

Lord, help me step out in obedience today…

_____
_____
_____

"But a man must examine himself, and in so doing he is to eat of the bread and drink of the cup." 1 Corinthians 11:28

Lord, I would like to share and repent…

_____
_____
_____

"For if you forgive others for their transgressions, your heavenly Father will also forgive you." Matthew 6:14

Lord, I need to forgive…

_____
_____
_____

"O taste and see that the LORD** is good; How blessed is the man who takes refuge in Him!"** Psalm 34:8

Lord, I praise You for today's blessings...

_____
_____
_____

"Ask, and it will be given to you; seek, and you will find; knock, and it will be opened to you." Matthew 7:7

Lord, hear my prayers …

_____
_____
_____
_____
_____
_____
_____

**"Open my eyes, that I may behold
Wonderful things from Your law."**
Psalm 119:18

Date: _____

Selected Bible Passage: "For the LORD God is a sun and shield; The LORD gives grace and glory; No good thing does He withhold from those who walk uprightly. O LORD of hosts. How blessed is the man who trusts in You!" Psalm 84:11-12

Reflections or Observations:

_____
_____
_____
_____

Inscribe the Selected Verse(s):

_____
_____
_____
_____
_____
_____
_____
_____
_____
_____
_____

· But He said, "On the contrary, blessed are those who hear the word of God and observe it." Luke 11:28

Lord, help me step out in obedience today…

_____
_____
_____

"But a man must examine himself, and in so doing he is to eat of the bread and drink of the cup." 1 Corinthians 11:28

Lord, I would like to share and repent…

_____
_____
_____

"For if you forgive others for their transgressions, your heavenly Father will also forgive you." Matthew 6:14

Lord, I need to forgive…

_____
_____
_____

"O taste and see that the LORD is good; How blessed is the man who takes refuge in Him!" Psalm 34:8

Lord, I praise You for today's blessings...

_____
_____
_____

"Ask, and it will be given to you; seek, and you will find; knock, and it will be opened to you." Matthew 7:7

Lord, hear my prayers …

_____
_____
_____
_____
_____
_____

> "Open my eyes, that I may behold
> Wonderful things from Your law."
> Psalm 119:18

Date: _____

Selected Bible Passage:
"And He has said to me, "My grace is sufficient for you, for power is perfected in weakness." Most gladly, therefore, I will rather boast about my weaknesses, so that the power of Christ may dwell in me."
2 Corinthians 12:9

Reflections or Observations:
_____
_____
_____
_____

Inscribe the Selected Verse(s):
_____
_____
_____
_____
_____
_____
_____
_____
_____
_____

But He said, "On the contrary, blessed are those who hear the word of God and observe it." Luke 11:28

Lord, help me step out in obedience today…

_____
_____
_____

"But a man must examine himself, and in so doing he is to eat of the bread and drink of the cup." 1 Corinthians 11:28

Lord, I would like to share and repent…

_____
_____
_____

"For if you forgive others for their transgressions, your heavenly Father will also forgive you." Matthew 6:14

Lord, I need to forgive…

_____
_____
_____

"O taste and see that the LORD is good; How blessed is the man who takes refuge in Him!" Psalm 34:8

Lord, I praise You for today's blessings…

_____
_____
_____

"Ask, and it will be given to you; seek, and you will find; knock, and it will be opened to you." Matthew 7:7

Lord, hear my prayers …

_____
_____
_____
_____
_____
_____

**"Open my eyes, that I may behold
Wonderful things from Your law."**
Psalm 119:18

Date: _____

Selected Bible Passage: "He shall say to them, 'Hear, O Israel, you are approaching the battle against your enemies today. Do not be fainthearted. Do not be afraid, or panic, or tremble before them, for the LORD your God is the one who goes with you, to fight for you against your enemies, to save you." Deuteronomy 20:4

Reflections or Observations:

_____
_____
_____

Inscribe the Selected Verse(s):

_____
_____
_____
_____
_____
_____
_____

But He said, "On the contrary, blessed are those who hear the word of God and observe it." Luke 11:28

Lord, help me step out in obedience today…

_____
_____
_____

"But a man must examine himself, and in so doing he is to eat of the bread and drink of the cup." 1 Corinthians 11:28

Lord, I would like to share and repent…

_____
_____
_____

"For if you forgive others for their transgressions, your heavenly Father will also forgive you." Matthew 6:14

Lord, I need to forgive…

_____
_____
_____

**"O taste and see that the LORD is good;
How blessed is the man who takes refuge in Him!"** Psalm 34:8

Lord, I praise You for today's blessings…

_____
_____
_____

"Ask, and it will be given to you; seek, and you will find; knock, and it will be opened to you." Matthew 7:7

Lord, hear my prayers …

_____
_____
_____
_____
_____
_____

**"Open my eyes, that I may behold
Wonderful things from Your law."**
Psalm 119:18

Date: _____

Selected Bible Passage: "Therefore, having been justified by faith, we have peace with God through our Lord Jesus Christ through whom also we have obtained our introduction by faith into this grace in which we stand; and we exult in hope of the glory of God."
Romans 5:1-2

Reflections or Observations:
_____
_____
_____
_____

Inscribe the Selected Verse(s):
_____
_____
_____
_____
_____
_____
_____
_____
_____
_____
_____

> **But He said, "On the contrary, blessed are those who hear the word of God and observe it."** Luke 11:28

Lord, help me step out in obedience today…

_____
_____
_____

> **"But a man must examine himself, and in so doing he is to eat of the bread and drink of the cup."** 1 Corinthians 11:28

Lord, I would like to share and repent…

_____
_____
_____

> **"For if you forgive others for their transgressions, your heavenly Father will also forgive you."** Matthew 6:14

Lord, I need to forgive…

_____
_____
_____

> **"O taste and see that the LORD is good;
> How blessed is the man who takes refuge in Him!"** Psalm 34:8

Lord, I praise You for today's blessings…

_____
_____
_____

> **"Ask, and it will be given to you; seek, and you will find; knock, and it will be opened to you."** Matthew 7:7

Lord, hear my prayers …

_____
_____
_____
_____
_____
_____

**"Open my eyes, that I may behold
Wonderful things from Your law."**
Psalm 119:18

Date: _____

Selected Bible Passage: "I will ask the Father, and He will give you another Helper, that He may be with you forever; *that is* the Spirit of truth, whom the world cannot receive, because it does not see Him or know Him, *but* you know Him because He abides with you and will be in you." John 14: 16-17

Reflections or Observations:
_____
_____
_____
_____
_____

Inscribe the Selected Verse(s):
_____
_____
_____
_____
_____
_____
_____
_____
_____
_____
_____

But He said, "On the contrary, blessed are those who hear the word of God and observe it." Luke 11:28

Lord, help me step out in obedience today…

_____
_____
_____

"But a man must examine himself, and in so doing he is to eat of the bread and drink of the cup." 1 Corinthians 11:28

Lord, I would like to share and repent…

_____
_____
_____

"For if you forgive others for their transgressions, your heavenly Father will also forgive you." Matthew 6:14

Lord, I need to forgive…

_____
_____
_____

"O taste and see that the LORD is good; How blessed is the man who takes refuge in Him!" Psalm 34:8

Lord, I praise You for today's blessings…

_____
_____
_____

"Ask, and it will be given to you; seek, and you will find; knock, and it will be opened to you." Matthew 7:7

Lord, hear my prayers …

_____
_____
_____
_____
_____
_____

> **"Open my eyes, that I may behold
> Wonderful things from Your law."**
> Psalm 119:18

Date: _____

Selected Bible Passage: "Peace I leave with you; My peace I give to you; not as the world gives do, I give to you. Do not let your heart be troubled, nor let it be fearful." John 14:27

Reflections or Observations:
_____
_____
_____
_____
_____

Inscribe the Selected Verse(s):
_____
_____
_____
_____
_____
_____
_____
_____
_____
_____
_____
_____

But He said, "On the contrary, blessed are those who hear the word of God and observe it." Luke 11:28

Lord, help me step out in obedience today…

_____
_____
_____

"But a man must examine himself, and in so doing he is to eat of the bread and drink of the cup." 1 Corinthians 11:28

Lord, I would like to share and repent…

_____
_____
_____

"For if you forgive others for their transgressions, your heavenly Father will also forgive you." Matthew 6:14

Lord, I need to forgive…

_____
_____
_____

"O taste and see that the LORD is good; How blessed is the man who takes refuge in Him!" Psalm 34:8

Lord, I praise You for today's blessings…

_____
_____
_____

"Ask, and it will be given to you; seek, and you will find; knock, and it will be opened to you." Matthew 7:7

Lord, hear my prayers …

_____
_____
_____
_____
_____
_____

**"Open my eyes, that I may behold
Wonderful things from Your law."**
Psalm 119:18

Date: _____

Selected Bible Passage: "But when He, the Spirit of truth, comes, He will guide you into all the truth; for He will not speak on His own initiative, but whatever He hears, He will speak; and He will disclose to you what is to come." John 16:13-14

Reflections or Observations:
_____
_____
_____
_____
_____

Inscribe the Selected Verse(s):
_____
_____
_____
_____
_____
_____
_____
_____
_____
_____
_____

But He said, "On the contrary, blessed are those who hear the word of God and observe it." Luke 11:28

Lord, help me step out in obedience today…

_____
_____
_____

"But a man must examine himself, and in so doing he is to eat of the bread and drink of the cup." 1 Corinthians 11:28

Lord, I would like to share and repent…

_____
_____
_____

"For if you forgive others for their transgressions, your heavenly Father will also forgive you." Matthew 6:14

Lord, I need to forgive…

_____
_____
_____

**"O taste and see that the LORD is good;
How blessed is the man who takes refuge in Him!"** Psalm 34:8

Lord, I praise You for today's blessings…

_____
_____
_____

"Ask, and it will be given to you; seek, and you will find; knock, and it will be opened to you." Matthew 7:7

Lord, hear my prayers …

_____
_____
_____
_____
_____
_____

> **"Open my eyes, that I may behold
> Wonderful things from Your law."**
> Psalm 119:18

Date: _____

Selected Bible Passage: "Rejoice in the Lord always; again, I will say, rejoice! Let your gentle *spirit* be known to all men. The Lord is near." Philippians 4: 4-5

Reflections or Observations:
_____
_____
_____
_____
_____

Inscribe the Selected Verse(s):
_____
_____
_____
_____
_____
_____
_____
_____
_____
_____
_____
_____

But He said, "On the contrary, blessed are those who hear the word of God and observe it." Luke 11:28

Lord, help me step out in obedience today...
___
___
___

"But a man must examine himself, and in so doing he is to eat of the bread and drink of the cup." 1 Corinthians 11:28

Lord, I would like to share and repent...
___
___
___

"For if you forgive others for their transgressions, your heavenly Father will also forgive you." Matthew 6:14

Lord, I need to forgive...
___
___
___

"O taste and see that the LORD** is good; How blessed is the man who takes refuge in Him!"** Psalm 34:8

Lord, I praise You for today's blessings...
___
___
___

"Ask, and it will be given to you; seek, and you will find; knock, and it will be opened to you." Matthew 7:7

Lord, hear my prayers ...
___
___
___
___
___
___

**"Open my eyes, that I may behold
Wonderful things from Your law."**
Psalm 119:18

Date: _____

Selected Bible Passage: "Be anxious for nothing, but in everything by prayer and supplication with thanksgiving let your requests be made known to God. And the peace of God, which surpasses all comprehension, will guard your hearts and your minds in Christ Jesus." Philippians 4: 6-7

Reflections or Observations:
_____
_____
_____
_____
_____

Inscribe the Selected Verse(s):
_____
_____
_____
_____
_____
_____
_____
_____
_____
_____
_____
_____
_____

But He said, "On the contrary, blessed are those who hear the word of God and observe it." Luke 11:28

Lord, help me step out in obedience today…

_____
_____
_____

"But a man must examine himself, and in so doing he is to eat of the bread and drink of the cup." 1 Corinthians 11:28

Lord, I would like to share and repent…

_____
_____
_____

"For if you forgive others for their transgressions, your heavenly Father will also forgive you." Matthew 6:14

Lord, I need to forgive…

_____
_____
_____

"O taste and see that the LORD is good;
How blessed is the man who takes refuge in Him!" Psalm 34:8

Lord, I praise You for today's blessings…

_____
_____
_____

"Ask, and it will be given to you; seek, and you will find; knock, and it will be opened to you." Matthew 7:7

Lord, hear my prayers …

_____
_____
_____
_____
_____
_____

**"Open my eyes, that I may behold
Wonderful things from Your law."**
Psalm 119:18

Date: _____

Selected Bible Passage: "Finally, brethren, whatever is true, whatever is honorable, whatever is right, whatever is pure, whatever is lovely, whatever is of good repute, if there is any excellence and if anything, worthy of praise, dwell on these things." Philippians 4:8

Reflections or Observations:
_____
_____
_____
_____
_____

Inscribe the Selected Verse(s):
_____
_____
_____
_____
_____
_____
_____
_____
_____
_____
_____

But He said, "On the contrary, blessed are those who hear the word of God and observe it." Luke 11:28

Lord, help me step out in obedience today…

___

"But a man must examine himself, and in so doing he is to eat of the bread and drink of the cup." 1 Corinthians 11:28

Lord, I would like to share and repent…

___

"For if you forgive others for their transgressions, your heavenly Father will also forgive you." Matthew 6:14

Lord, I need to forgive…

___

"O taste and see that the LORD is good;
How blessed is the man who takes refuge in Him!" Psalm 34:8

Lord, I praise You for today's blessings...

___

"Ask, and it will be given to you; seek, and you will find; knock, and it will be opened to you." Matthew 7:7

Lord, hear my prayers …

**"Open my eyes, that I may behold
Wonderful things from Your law."**
Psalm 119:18

Date: _____

Selected Bible Passage: "Yet those who wait for the LORD will gain new strength; They will mount up *with* wings like eagles, they will run and not get tired, they will walk and not become weary." Isaiah 40:31

Reflections or Observations:
_____
_____
_____
_____
_____

Inscribe the Selected Verse(s):
_____
_____
_____
_____
_____
_____
_____
_____
_____
_____
_____
_____
_____

But He said, "On the contrary, blessed are those who hear the word of God and observe it." Luke 11:28

Lord, help me step out in obedience today…

_____
_____
_____

"But a man must examine himself, and in so doing he is to eat of the bread and drink of the cup." 1 Corinthians 11:28

Lord, I would like to share and repent…

_____
_____
_____

"For if you forgive others for their transgressions, your heavenly Father will also forgive you." Matthew 6:14

Lord, I need to forgive…

_____
_____
_____

**"O taste and see that the LORD is good;
How blessed is the man who takes refuge in Him!"** Psalm 34:8

Lord, I praise You for today's blessings…

_____
_____
_____

"Ask, and it will be given to you; seek, and you will find; knock, and it will be opened to you." Matthew 7:7

Lord, hear my prayers …

_____
_____
_____
_____
_____
_____
_____

**"Open my eyes, that I may behold
Wonderful things from Your law."**
Psalm 119:18

Date: _____

Selected Bible Passage: "The LORD is near to all who call upon Him, to all who call upon Him in truth. He will fulfill the desire of those who fear Him; He will also hear their cry and will save them." Psalms 145:18-19

Reflections or Observations:
_____
_____
_____
_____

Inscribe the Selected Verse(s):
_____
_____
_____
_____
_____
_____
_____
_____
_____
_____
_____

But He said, "On the contrary, blessed are those who hear the word of God and observe it." Luke 11:28

Lord, help me step out in obedience today…
_____
_____
_____

"But a man must examine himself, and in so doing he is to eat of the bread and drink of the cup." 1 Corinthians 11:28

Lord, I would like to share and repent…
_____
_____
_____

"For if you forgive others for their transgressions, your heavenly Father will also forgive you." Matthew 6:14

Lord, I need to forgive…
_____
_____
_____

"O taste and see that the LORD is good; How blessed is the man who takes refuge in Him!" Psalm 34:8

Lord, I praise You for today's blessings…
_____
_____
_____

"Ask, and it will be given to you; seek, and you will find; knock, and it will be opened to you." Matthew 7:7

Lord, hear my prayers …
_____
_____
_____
_____
_____
_____

Lord,

You are a Wonderful Counselor, Mighty God, Everlasting Father, Prince of Peace, and God of Hope. (Isaiah 9:6) "How remarkable is that?!" We are never alone. He is always with us. He is our beloved Immanuel (Matt 1:21).

You are our Savior who shines a bright Light to the World!

"She will bear a Son; and you shall call His name Jesus, for He will save His people from their sins." (Matthew 1:21) My heart rejoices when I think of you, Jesus, as my Savior, who rescued me out of the pit of darkness. You were crucified at the Cross on my behalf. You cleansed me from all of my sins when I humbly brought them all to your attention, surrendered my heart and pinned my repentance to the Cross. I have been set free for eternity.

You chose the ordinary, the unexpected and sinners like me! Your heart is pure and willing to save us all. **"Thanks be to God for His indescribable gift!"** 2 Corinthians 9:15. Lord, you are our only source of true Hope and my Salvation. You are an indescribable gift to my heart and soul.

I wait expectantly for miracles to unfold throughout the day. We all have a fresh start at sunrise! Yes, you are the source of my confidence as I make decisions all day long. I am not trusting any of my circumstances or people who are in my sphere of influence.

I am trusting you alone, Lord.

Life circumstances abruptly change and relationships either evolve over time or change, a few of our friends walk away unexpectedly and others lose contact when they move away geographically.

But God…

I can trust you to be always faithful. Your character never changes regardless of the season of the year. Lord, you never cease to exist, never disappoints and your love never fades away. How incredible it is to fall in love with Jesus all over again as we move forward in a new chapter of our lives, a fresh start this year. Lord, relieve our troubles of our hearts and free us from anguish always (Psalm 25:17). Hear our prayers and comfort us today!

Let us embrace a new season, a new dance, a new song of praise as we all move forward into our new season this year!

In Jesus' name, I bravely pray and boldly praise my King of kings.

Amen.

ABOUT THE AUTHOR

Adriana Morales-Spokane was born in Venezuela. She relocated to the United States at a young age and lived in Florida for twenty-six years. She visits her family and friends in Miami yearly and delights herself with Cuban meals.

Adriana now lives with her husband in Collierville, Tennessee and works full-time in a leadership role with the State.

Adriana enjoys adult coloring, creative Bible journaling, piano playing and blogging for KeynotesinHisPresence.org
What is her favorite time of day? Adriana enjoys waking up at sunrise to read her Bible, does her devotionals, and prayers.

For over a decade, Adriana delights in serving faithfully in discipleship communities. Her motto is "Truth in action." She is passionate about The Great Commission.

Professionally, Adriana has been in the mental health field for over twenty-six years and has faithfully served children, adolescents and their families as well as adults with intellectual disabilities (ID) and Autism Spectrum Disorder (ASD). She worked as a Licensed Mental Health Counselor (LMHC), and registered Clinical Supervisor with the State of Florida Board prior to her relocation. Adriana is also a Board-Certified Behavior Analyst and a Licensed Clinical Psychologist in the State of Tennessee.

KeynotesinHisPresence.org captures Adriana's life journey. She is mindful of her walk with Jesus Christ 'everywhere' she goes. She adores her Savior and Redeemer.

Adriana's email: KeynotesinHisPresence@gmail.com

Subscribe to Blog: KeynotesinHisPresence.org
Join the Public Page on Facebook: Keynotes in His Presence.

'Bible Reading Journal' series available on Amazon.com

Volume 1
Bible Reading Journal: Growing Closer to God One Day at a Time.

Volume 2
Bible Reading Journal: Rest and Be Refreshed.

Volume 3
Bible Reading Journal: Praise and Be Content.

All of these journals will be published by Spring 2019.

There will be seven volumes for the Bible Reading Journal series by the end of 2019. Note, publication date is subject to change.

Bible Reading Journal: Rest and Be Refreshed.
"Your Word is a lamp to my feet. And a light to my path."
Psalm 119:105

No part of this publication may be reproduced, stored in a retrieval system or transmitted in any form by any means, electronic, mechanical, photocopy, recording, or otherwise, without the prior permission of the author, except as provided for by USA copyright law.

Cover and Book design: Adriana Morales-Spokane, 2019.

Made in the USA
Middletown, DE
02 February 2019